today you grieve.

tomorrow you heal.

-- adrian michael

TITLES YOU MIGHT LIKE
BY
ADRIAN MICHAEL

--

loamexpressions

blinking cursor

notes of a denver native son

blackmagic

lovehues

notes from a gentle man

blooming hearts

book of her book of she

Published by Creative Genius Publishing—
an imprint of lovasté | Denver, CO

To contact the author visit adrianmichaelgreen.com

ISBN-13: 978-1983825965
ISBN-10: 1983825964

Printed in the United States of America

FOR HEART'S THAT ACHE.

for ellison.

for hearts that ache.

try not to pull the sadness from your eyes
in order to pretend like you're all good.
  -- adrian michael

for hearts that ache.

look at sadness, dear heart,
as beautiful unhappiness sent
to shake you. not harm you.
  -- adrian michael

for hearts that ache.

how can anyone ever prepare for heartache?
and how can we begin to heal and put ourselves
back together again?

no matter what happens, trust your process.
we all grieve differently. what works for you may
not work for others. but when you situate yourself
to feel, your road will reveal itself. there is no
blueprint or timeline. you will be fine one minute
and a mess the next. you're open. you're exposed.
soon it gets easier and you'll look back

less broken.

-- *adrian michael*

for hearts that ache.

emotionally unavailable.
spiritually busy.
weeping.
weeping.
weeping.
   -- adrian michael

for hearts that ache.

mourning you.
still.
some days are easier.
it's when i hear your name
that sets my soul
in spin cycle
all over
again.
  -- adrian michael

for hearts that ache.

that moment when it gets to be too much.
feels too much. it's overwhelming. that's when
you choose to fight. to stay. to be honest and try.

you
will
get
through
this.
  -- adrian michael

for hearts that ache.

and when you're gentle with yourself
the hard edges of the world get softer.
  -- adrian michael

for hearts that ache.

healing can happen in a single moment.
   -- adrian michael

for hearts that ache.

*begging for acceptance teaches you
how to break in half. loving who you are
teaches you how to stay whole.*
  -- adrian michael

for hearts that ache.

heal yourself. tell yourself the words
no one has ever told you. tell yourself
what you need to hear.
  -- adrian michael

for hearts that ache.

pour love into every part of your being.
that way you're always overflowing.
  -- adrian michael

for hearts that ache.

soak yourself in love. this is not for others.

this is for you.

-- adrian michael

23

for hearts that ache.

save yourself.
be your own hero.
be your own savior.
be your own guru.
be your own healer.
be your own well.
be everything
you need to be okay.
  -- adrian michael

for hearts that ache.

just because you love them doesn't
mean you should be with them.
  -- adrian michael

for hearts that ache.

you are so loved.
you are so abundantly loved.
  -- adrian michael

for hearts that ache.

leave people and places that try to hurt you.
  -- adrian michael

for hearts that ache.

they will regret passing you up.
and you will thank them.
  -- adrian michael

for hearts that ache.

relationships can be perfect storms—
the best ones happen when
you don't see them coming.
  -- adrian michael

for hearts that ache.

remember:
water heals.
stay soft.
  -- adrian michael

for hearts that ache.

you are someone's best dream.

-- adrian michael

for hearts that ache.

honor grief.
sit in it.
let it tell you
where it hurts.
  -- adrian michael

for hearts that ache.

open up your heart.
it's time.
  -- adrian michael

for hearts that ache.

loving yourself isn't about trying to make someone want you back. loving yourself is about coming home. especially when you've been away too long.

-- adrian michael

for hearts that ache.

it's okay to be all up in your feelings.
swim in them. lay under them like you're
moon bathing. the more you spend time
with your heart, the better you learn
how to love yourself.
  -- adrian michael

for hearts that ache.

do what's best for you even if no one understands.
  -- adrian michael

for hearts that ache.

treat yourself

better.

-- adrian michael

for hearts that ache.

once and always yours.
  -- adrian michael

for hearts that ache.

your heart will beat over 100,000 times today.
don't waste any of its energy on people and things
that will try and break it. protect your heart.
  -- adrian michael

for hearts that ache.

strong relationships exist when people acknowledge
their struggles, actively work on them, and love on
each other especially in moments when it hurts.
  -- adrian michael

for hearts that ache.

stop searching for a home in people
who won't give you a key.
  -- adrian michael

for hearts that ache.

escape to places where no one knows your name.
break free from confinement and control. go to a
coffee shop, bookstore, mountain top, a pier on the
beach, favorite spot in the woods, close your eyes
and be with yourself. it doesn't matter. get away.
retreat from time to time. take care of your needs.

-- adrian michael

for hearts that ache.

and while you're talking about
    how they broke your heart;
    how they did you wrong;
    how they lost a good thing;
    how they left too soon;
you're healing yourself.
  -- adrian michael

for hearts that ache.

please don't judge yourself.
you're trying to put yourself
back together.
  -- adrian michael

for hearts that ache.

here's the thing about loving another person:
you won't know if you're any good at it until
you put yourself out there.

yes it's scary. yes you could get hurt.

but you could also feel the most incredible rush
and stumble across the people meant to teach you
how to love and what it means to fully live.
  -- adrian michael

for hearts that ache.

and when the storm passes
you will be stronger.
you will be wiser.
you will be bolder.
you will be healed.
you will be free.
  -- adrian michael

for hearts that ache.

to truly heal
break old habits.
  -- adrian michael

for hearts that ache.

you get to choose
who you give yourself to.
you get to choose
to keep all of yourself
to yourself.

  -- adrian michael

for hearts that ache.

when it starts to ache
you're healing.
  -- adrian michael

for hearts that ache.

self love is not selfish. it is necessary.
  -- adrian michael

for hearts that ache.

i'm sorry they hurt you.
  -- adrian michael

for hearts that ache.

today was hard.
but you made it.
  -- adrian michael

for hearts that ache.

their biggest mistake was not putting you first.
  -- adrian michael

for hearts that ache.

take care of yourself.

even fire gets tired of burning.

-- adrian michael

for hearts that ache.

all that weight isn't yours.
let go.
 -- adrian michael

for hearts that ache.

loss is part of life.
and losing loved ones
hurts bone deep.
grieve slowly.
hate the world if you must.
you will deny and repress; feel angry
and depressed; grow through it. accept.

they may be gone but they're always with you
as long as you keep their names on your lips.
  -- adrian michael

for hearts that ache.

anger has a hold of you.
remove it from your heart.
  -- adrian michael

for hearts that ache.

half love no one.
especially yourself.
  -- adrian michael

for hearts that ache.

learn to accept.
or learn to suffer.
you choose.
   -- adrian michael

for hearts that ache.

this time
        put your happiness first.
        don't let them get away with it.
        call them out.
        ignore their existence.
        don't think it was your fault.
        protect your heart.
    -- adrian michael

for hearts that ache.

pick yourself up.
piece by peace.
  -- adrian michael

for hearts that ache.

be the love you've always wanted.
  -- adrian michael

for hearts that ache.

evolve.
the skin shed
share a buried
home. and those
bones, dust.
   -- adrian michael

for hearts that ache.

you can't force the sun to rise.
it just happens. your sun is coming.

and when it does
it will be

epic.

-- adrian michael

for hearts that ache.

heal, dear heart.
then and only then
will you realize
how magic you are.
  -- adrian michael

for hearts that ache.

it's okay if they don't stay.
someone else is meant for you.
  -- adrian michael

for hearts that ache.

sometimes
solitude
is the best
company.
  -- adrian michael

for hearts that ache.

at a crossroad, a kind soul asked aloud,
"which way shall i turn? which way is best?"

quietly the universe responded,
"go until it feels like home."
  -- adrian michael

for hearts that ache.

the hurting
the healing
both require
the same
medicine.
  -- adrian michael

for hearts that ache.

it's okay to feel.
let yourself grieve.
  -- adrian michael

for hearts that ache.

you're the kind of soul anyone would be lucky to
be with. and you don't even know it. the great ones
never do.

  -- adrian michael

for hearts that ache.

how freeing it is
being with someone
who gets you.
  -- adrian michael

for hearts that ache.

leaves fall for a reason.
  -- adrian michael

for hearts that ache.

beautifully broken.
beautifully whole.
  -- adrian michael

for hearts that ache.

document the times you are happiest.
notice what you're doing. who you're with.

this is your flow.
this is your zen.
this is your ma'at.
this is your path.
  -- adrian michael

for hearts that ache.

*you are sad today. you keep being reminded over
and over again of how your life might be different
if things would have gone your way. instead, the
truth feels colder today. need i remind you that
happiness and sadness are two parts of the same
process. and right now, you are on your way back
towards...no. i can't give you a silver lining. no
motivation. to see the upside. right now, i'll just sit
with you. feel with you. be with you. cry with you.
be all that you need right now.
in this moment. take all the time necessary.
for i am sad today, too.*

   -- adrian michael

for hearts that ache.

love you gently. you're still healing.
  -- adrian michael

for hearts that ache.

when do you have time to cry when you are hold-ing tears for others? when do you grieve? who cries for you when you can't cry for you?

-- *adrian michael*

for hearts that ache.

we're all healing from something.
  -- adrian michael

for hearts that ache.

hold on, beautiful. better days are coming.
  -- adrian michael

for hearts that ache.

you are the one who is
capable enough,
strong enough,
deep enough,
soft enough,
to love yourself
better than
anyone else.
  -- adrian michael

for hearts that ache.

love is a process
that sends you
on a long walk
back to yourself.
  -- adrian michael

for hearts that ache.

dress your wounds.
clean them with sorrow.
wash the pain with salt.
turn your scars into honey.
drizzle the sweet sadness
into a hole and cover it up.
walk away. let go. move on.
  -- adrian michael

for hearts that ache.

be sad. and be strong.
be sad. and be loud.
be sad. and be hard.
be sad. and be firm.
be sad. and be soft.
be sad. and be quiet.
be sad. and stay
as long as you want.

give yourself permission
to open your heart.
let the rain out.
let the rain out.
let the rain out.
  -- adrian michael

for hearts that ache.

vengeance is in finding happiness.
not in waging war.
  -- adrian michael

for hearts that ache.

you're not broken.
you're unfinished.
you're millions
of puzzle pieces
searching
for the meaning
of each piece.
  -- adrian michael

for hearts that ache.

you once thought
you'd never
breathe again.

now look at you
breathing again.
-- adrian michael

Made in the USA
Monee, IL
18 July 2020